Artificial Intelligence in Healthcare, BFSI: Jobs, Threats, Challenges, and the Solutions ahead in a world of uncertain times.

From my Personal Experiences in Face Matching Software

by Akash V.P.

Artificial Intelligence by Akash V P

Artificial Intelligence by Akash V.P.

Cover by Akash V.P.

ISBN: 9781099319365

For any book orders from the author

contact amazingpublishedbooks@gmail.com

About me

The author is an IT Engineer from one of the topmost Engineering Institute (VJTI) where his final year project was based on IOT. He worked in Oracle, for clients like Sumitomo Bank and Silicon Valley Bank. He is a speaker on subjects like Chess and Mathematics. He would be coming up with a few books on AI based on his experience.

amazon.com/author/akashvp

amazingpublishedbooks@gmail.com

Like Facebook page - Artificial Intelligence Face Matching Page

Linkedin - Akash

Disclaimer

The author has stated some of his views and opinions in this book. There may be some information which may be viewed differently by readers as per their selective reading, knowledge, emotions, nationality and other psychological biases, etc. This is also to state that the author doesn't discriminate people based on their community, nationality or any other division/category. This is the first book written and published by the author.

INDEX

Bonus!

Wouldn't it be nice to know when my paperback books are launched at a discount? Well now is your chance!

Go to the below link For Instant Access!
http://

Simply as a 'Thank you for downloading this book, I would like to give you full access to an exclusive service that will email you notifications my paperback books are launched at a discount. If you are someone who is interested in saving money and getting technology books at a discount, then simple click the link for FREE access.

INTRODUCTION

Face matching... 78% matched. I was shocked. The AI based software showed a match between my face photograph six years earlier and today's selfie . Though most people look similar after adulthood for a decade, this isn't a case for me. I weighed 102 kgs (225 lbs) in 2013 whereas in 2019 I am a lean guy with 80 kgs (176 lbs) of weight. Also I have a thick mustache with a different hairstyle and facial features (including beard) but six years ago I was chubby and the photograph has no facial hair.

This is the growth in technology where the software can be more accurate than humans (many friends, relatives couldn't recognize me after years), but the software is on spot. Though not 100% but still a 78% match means that two different looking photos can be of the same person. The technology used by the software will be discussed later in the chapters.

Flashback

It was in a session arranged in our organization that I got introduced to AI aka Artificial Intelligence. The speaker Utpal, now my mentor, appeared like a magician delivering his presentation. With traffic prediction to detection of skin cancers to a program beating the best human player at the brain challenging game of Go, the software can do a variety of tasks. The audience was also dumb folded with the

new knowledge shared with them. Some of the questions were
A. Can this be applied to the stock market and help me make money,
B. If everyone come to know that a particular road has lesser traffic, everyone traveling through an alternate road /highway would soon use this and there would be traffic.
Soon there was laughter filled in the room over these questions asked with the inquisitive nature of a child. Thus I was introduced to this amazing world of AI and became excited about the intelligent machines and the future.

I didn't stop at one session like most of the others, but went on to attend each and every session conducted on this topic at our organization. In the process I also ended befriending the speaker who in turned mentored me with his knowledge and guidance. In case you are not aware of Utpal, he is a speaker on the AI topic in conferences all around the world. He gets invitations to be the guest speaker on Data Science, Machine Learning and related topics. At this point of writing he has already spoken at Miami, Abu Dhabi, Shanghai, Singapore and various other AI conferences in the country and around the world. He also heads the department of Artificial intelligence in our organization and has great experience in the industry developing AI based applications.
Also around the same time I was working on the project of Face matching for KYC purposes. The technology is based on AI/ML which increased my curiosity further in this topic. I

also happened to attend the conference where Siraj Raval (the YouTube star on AI) was the guest speaker.

I am writing this book to share my knowledge and experience about the face matching technology, and the future in which we would be living. My engineering college project was also based on ubiquitous computing and IOT which are related to AI. Little did I knew how crucial these fields would shape up in the future.

Sometimes I feel like the Neo from Matrix living in a technology world along with the physical world.

I have put in my best efforts to make sure that this book is suitable for both those curious to learn about artificial intelligence as well as for the experts no doors you have already been through this journey at want to learn more about this so I have made sure to include the best of my knowledge from my personal experience and also from my extensive reading.

Thanks,
Akash V.P.

Chapter 1.

Face Matching Software

This face matching software which compares the faces of two individuals. It is basically used to know whether that person is the same one whose account opening. And a way to avoid a fraud or fraudulent transaction in the future. So the software extracts the face of a person from there a photo identity card for unauthorized ID card and a selfie of that person is taken then match between two faces is found by using this particular software. The output is a particular number like 60% 80% or 30% which tells us know whether this particular match is good or not. This match percentage tells us whether we should go ahead or not and the bank account should be made for that person or not.

Additional factor of authentication along with manual verification helps Bank in eliminating errors while onboarding the customer.

The software also has additional features like the OCR it is optical character recognition which captures the address of a person and it can be edited in the application.

There are a few more features for which various API are used. This face matching app can be mounted as an SDK (software development kit) on top of the main app or the APIs of face matching have to be enabled to be used with the main app.

The following is a very simplified architecture diagram of the software. This software can be deployed on premises or by using cloud computing (like Azure, AWS, Google Cloud etc.)

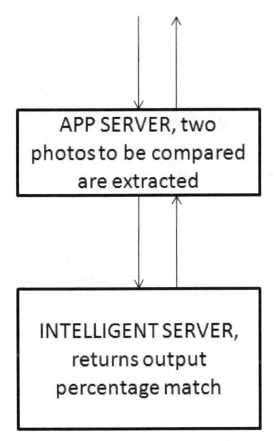

Figure 1 Simplified Architecture diagram for Face Matching Software

The above two servers have middleware installed on the **docker**. The **technology stack** consisting of Tesseract, Tomcat, Java 1.8+ and many more softwares.

The servers have specific requirements for Hard Disk or SSD, RAM, and CPU depending on the load expected. As the business transactions increase these requirements also have to be modified. It's better to use **cloud computing** (**PAAS**) because the capacity can be changed as and when required much faster than a traditional infrastructure network.

The API (request response) works as below:
The two photos to be compared are extracted in the app server and the data is sent to the intelligent server. The intelligent server compares them and sends a percentage match to the app server.

This app server then send this value to the main app where it can be seen by an authorized person using that app.

The photo matching can be done from an image or a video of that person where their face can be seen.

The intelligent server contains a CNN (Convolutional Neural Network) which learns and becomes more intelligent as more data sets are fed into it. The other popular neural networks are RNN and

LSTM, on which self driving cars run.

By learning more about this application, I came to know that how lesser known companies/startups can create amazing softwares in their specialized field even better than the top 5 technology companies in the world can create.

Note - The DB server is installed on the same server on which the App server is installed. We can keep the DB server separate from the app server, for which the architecture diagram will vary.
The DB server will be used for metadata.

Chapter 2

AI in Healthcare

Artificial intelligence (AI) in healthcare is making utilization of intricate formulas as well as software programs to approximate human cognition in the analysis of difficult clinical information. Especially, AI is the capacity for computer system algorithms to estimated conclusions sans direct human input.

What differentiates AI technology from standard modern technologies in wellness treatment is the capability to acquire details, process it and also offer a well-defined result to the end-user. AI algorithms behave in a different way from humans in two means:

(1) formulas are actual: if you set an objective, the formula cannot change itself and also only understand what is has been told explicitly,

(2) and algorithms are black boxes; formulas can anticipate incredibly accurate, but not the cause or the why.

Medical institutions such as The Mayo Facility, Memorial Sloan Kettering Cancer Facility, Massachusetts General Hospital, and National Health And Wellness Solution, have actually developed AI algorithms for their departments. Large innovation companies such as IBM as well as Google, and also startups such as Welltok as well as Ayasdi, have also created AI formulas for healthcare.

Furthermore, hospitals are looking to AI remedies to support functional campaigns that boost price conserving, enhance person contentment, and also please their staffing and labor force demands.

History Research in the 1960s as well as 1970s produced the initial problem-solving program, or professional system, known as Dendral. While it was made for applications in organic chemistry, it supplied the basis for a succeeding system MYCIN, considered one of the most substantial very early uses of artificial intelligence in medication. MYCIN and also various other systems such as INTERNIST-1 as well as CASNET did not achieve routine usage by experts.

The 1980s and 1990s brought the spreading of the microcomputer and brand-new levels of network connection. Throughout this time, there was an acknowledgment by researchers and developers that AI systems in healthcare should be created to suit the lack of ideal information and also develop on the know-how of physicians. Approaches including fuzzy collection theory, Bayesian networks, as well as artificial neural networks, have actually been applied to smart computing systems in healthcare.

Medical and also technological advancements taking place over this half-century duration that have allowed the development healthcare-related applications of AI include:

- Improvements in calculating power causing much faster data collection and also data handling

- Raised quantity and also schedule of health-related data from personal and healthcare-related gadgets

- Growth of genomic sequencing data sources
- Extensive execution of digital health document systems
- Improvements in all-natural language handling as well as computer vision, making it possible for devices to replicate human perceptual procedures
- Improved the precision of robot-assisted surgery

Current study
Various specialized in medicine have revealed a rise in research relating to AI.

Radiology
The radiology seminar Radiological Culture of North America has actually applied presentations on AI in imaging during its annual meeting. The emergence of AI modern technology in radiology is viewed as a hazard by some specialists, as the technology can attain improvements in specific analytical metrics in isolated cases, as opposed to professionals.

Imaging
Current advancements have actually recommended using AI to describe and examine the outcome of maxillo-facial surgery or the

evaluation of slit individuals therapy in relation to facial beauty or age appearance.

Telehealth

The rise of Telemedicine, has actually shown the rise of possible AI applications. The capacity to keep an eye on clients using AI might enable the interaction of details to physicians when possible disease activity might have occurred. A wearable gadget might permit consistent monitoring of a person and likewise permit the ability to see changes that might be much less distinct by humans.

Electronic Health And Wellness Records

Electronic health records are critical to the digitalization and also details spread of the healthcare sector. Logging all of this information comes with its own issues like cognitive overload and burnout for customers. EHR programmers are now automating a lot of the process and also beginning to utilize natural language handling (NLP) devices to improve this process. One research study carried out by the Centerstone research study institute found that predictive modeling of EHR data has actually accomplished 70- 72% accuracy in predicting personalized treatment action at standard. Suggesting making use of an AI device that checks EHR data it can quite properly anticipate the program of condition in a person.

Sector

The succeeding objective of huge based wellness business combining with other health and wellness companies, enable higher wellness information availability. Greater health and wellness data may enable more execution of AI formulas.

A huge component of industry emphasis of implementation of AI in the healthcare field remains in the scientific decision assistance systems. As the amount of information increases, AI decision support group end up being a lot more efficient. Many companies are checking out the opportunities of the incorporation of huge information in the health care industry.

The adhering to are instances of large business that have actually added to AI formulas for usage in healthcare.

IBM

IBM's Watson Oncology remains in development at Memorial Sloan Kettering Cancer Cells Center and also Cleveland Clinic. IBM is likewise collaborating with CVS Health and wellness on AI applications in chronic condition therapy as well as with Johnson & Johnson on analysis of clinical documents to locate brand-new connections for medicine advancement.

Microsoft

Microsoft's Hanover job, in collaboration with Oregon Health and wellness & Science University's Knight Cancer Institute, evaluates clinical research study to anticipate the most efficient cancer medicine treatment choices for clients. Other jobs include clinical picture analysis of growth progression as well as the advancement of programmable cells.

Google

Google's DeepMind platform is being made use of by the UK National Health and wellness Solution to spot certain wellness dangers via information collected via a mobile app. A 2nd job with the NHS includes evaluation of medical images collected from NHS people to create computer system vision algorithms to find malignant tissues.

Intel

Intel's equity capital arm Intel Resources recently purchased startup Lumiata which uses AI to create and also determine at-risk patients care alternatives.

Startups

identRx is the initial totally automated drug confirmation and also dispensing tool, making use of AI to validate and also determine pill in real time, with an accuracy above 99%. The gadget has actually been under advancement my PerceptiMed Inc. as well as is currently readily available for drug stores in the US.

IDx's very first service, IDx-DR founded by Michael Abramoff, is the very first and also just FDA authorized AI system for the autonomous discovery of diabetic retinopathy. As an autonomous, AI-based system, IDx-DR is distinct in that it makes an evaluation without the requirement for a medical professional to additionally interpret the photo or results, making it useful by healthcare companies who might not usually be associated with eye care. IDx

is a leading AI diagnostics business on an objective to transform the top quality, ease of access, as well as affordability of healthcare globally.

Kheiron Medical established deep learning software to identify breast cancers cells in mammograms.

Predictive Medical Technologies makes use of intensive treatment system data to identify people likely to suffer heart occurrences.

Modernizing Medicine makes use of understanding collected from healthcare experts as well as client outcome information to suggest treatments. "Thoughtful AI Laboratory" makes use of grid cell, area cell and path assimilation with equipment discovering for the navigation of blind people.

Infermedica's free mobile application Symptomate is the top-rated sign checker in Google Play. The business likewise released the initial AI-based voice aide sign mosaic for three significant voice platforms: Amazon.com Alexa, Microsoft Cortana, as well as Google Aide.

A team related to the College of Arizona as well as backed by BPU

Holdings started teaming up on a functional tool to keep an eye on anxiety and delirium in healthcare facility clients, particularly those with Mental deterioration. The AI used in the brand-new innovation- Senior's Virtual Aide- goes an action past as well as is configured to imitate as well as understand human emotions (synthetic emotional intelligence). Medical professionals dealing with the project have suggested that in enhancement to evaluating emotions, the application can be utilized to supply companionship to patients in the kind of tiny talk, relaxing songs, as well as even lighting modifications to control anxiety.

Other

Digital professional apps like Babylon Wellness's General Practitioner handy, Ada Health And Wellness, and Your.MD use AI to give clinical appointment based upon personal clinical background and usual clinical knowledge. Individuals report their signs into the app, which makes use of speech recognition to contrast against a database of ailments. Babylon then uses an advised activity, taking into consideration the customer's case history. Business owners in healthcare have actually been properly making use of seven service design archetypes to take AI option to the marketplace. These archetypes depends on the value create for the target user (e.g. patient focus vs. doctor and payer emphasis) and also value capturing systems (e.g. providing information or connecting stakeholders).

Ramifications

Making use of AI is forecasted to decrease medical prices as there will certainly be extra precision in medical diagnosis as well as much better predictions in the therapy plan along with more avoidance of disease.

Other future uses for AI consist of Brain-computer Interfaces (BCI) which are predicted to assist those with problem moving, talking or with a spine cable injury. The BCIs will use AI to aid these people action and also interact by deciphering neural triggers

Digital nursing assistants are forecasted to come to be much more common and these will make use of AI to respond to person's questions as well as help lower unnecessary hospital visits. They will certainly be helpful as they are available 24/7 as well as may at some point be able to offer wellness contact using AI as well as voice

The U.S. Information Staff writes that in the close to future, doctors who use AI will certainly "win out" the medical professionals who don't. AI will certainly not change healthcare workers but instead enable them even more time for bed side cares.

Expanding Like Developing Countries

With a rise in the use of AI, more care may appear to those in developing nations. AI remains to increase in its abilities and also as it is able to translate radiology, it might have the ability to identify even more people with the requirement for much less medical professionals as there is a scarcity in most of these countries The objective of AI is to teach others worldwide, which will then cause better treatment, and also ultimately higher international health and wellness. Utilizing AI in establishing nations that do not have the resources will certainly diminish the requirement for outsourcing and can utilize AI to boost individual treatment. All-natural language processing, as well as maker discovering are being used for directing cancer therapies in areas such as Thailand, China as well as India. Researchers educated

an AI application to make use of NLP to mine via patient documents, and also supply therapy. The supreme decision made by the AI application agreed with specialist decisions 90% of the time.

Chapter 3

Chatbots

Chatbot is AI based and is often used to reply to customer texts in real time.

Advantages of Chatbots

Chatbots are very beneficial for a great deal of different applications-from simple user contact, to addressing questions, and also even aiding the sales process along.

Among the largest benefits of utilizing Chatbots is that you can have less real staff members, due to the fact that chatbots can care for a lot of issues that could occupy time from paid employees. This frees up paid employees for more important jobs, as well as permits them to have even more time to aid customers with significant concerns. This advantages consumers, also, because they can get the answer to questions and assist with issues much faster than they may if they wound up getting in touch with customer support through traditional methods.

Bots can also supply you incredibly valuable details concerning your consumers if you log those conversations as well as evaluate them, because you can see the kinds of questions they are asking. Never neglect those logs as a way to find out even more concerning them.

Chatbot Limitations/Drawbacks

Naturally, chatbots have a few downsides, too. No technology is perfect, as well as bots are no exception. The most significant disadvantage is that expert system, despite how progressed it might be, is not yet at the degree that can change actual people. This certainly causes failing to help consumers in some cases, which may wind up frustrating the user enough that they leave your website. This is unusual, yet it can take place, so you should make sure your chatbot can guide consumers to live assistance when required. Numerous bots are improperly programmed due to the fact that they have been rushed to market to benefit from the rise in chatbot use, so you should be on the lookout for this, also. The most affordable solution isn't constantly the most effective, so it's vital that you examine your chatbot extensively to ensure there are not a problem with it that could end up discouraging your consumers.

Are Chatbots Appropriate For You?
Chatbots aren't right for each organization. If you discover that you don't have a great deal of call with customers typically, you might not need a chatbot. Yet, on the other hand, if you do have a lot of call with clients, or if you locate you have a lot of shopping cart abandonment or your clients often tend to ask a great deal of concerns or require extra aid, a chatbot simply could be ideal for your needs.

Right here are some scenarios where a chatbot might benefit your organization:

1. Your client service representatives are overwhelmed. If you find that your representatives are overwhelmed by the volume helpful demands you obtain daily, especially if there are easy demands that could quickly be taken care of by a bot, it makes perfect feeling for you to use one.

2. You have a high price of buying cart desertion. If you discover that a great deal of people are deserting their purchasing carts or leaving your site without exchanging e-mail subscribers or buyers, a chatbot could help by asking the consumer what went wrong when they attempt to leave your website, and afterwards assist them with the process so they can complete the conversion.

3. Consumers maintain asking the same inquiries over as well as over. Let's encounter it, consumers hardly ever read F.A.Q. pages. Sometimes you may question, "Why even bother having a F.A.Q. page? It looks like no one reviews them!" That is true. Yet chatbots are a terrific method to get more people to find out the solution to basic questions without squandering you or your agents' time. You can configure common inquiries right into your bot and also allow it respond to those inquiries.

4. Your organization is oriented towards service. If you're in a sector

that is infamously service-centric, such as the travel sector, for example, chatbots can go a long method towards assisting customers obtain help while alleviating some of the initial work that representatives may or else need to handle.

These are just a few examples, yet ideally you're beginning to obtain an idea of whether a crawler might be a good suitable for your organization.

Ways to Make Use of Chatbots

There are many methods to utilize chatbots for organization, and companies are considering brand-new, ingenious means to use them regularly. Let's take a look at a few methods chatbots can benefit your organization.

Web content Delivery

A lot of companies are using chatbot technology to supply content in a new an intriguing means. Sites such as CNN are sending out intriguing write-ups to visitors with messaging apps.

Considering that a lot of individuals are using messenger apps like Facebook and also Kik on a regular basis, providing content straight to the systems they're currently using just makes sense.

This enables business to reach viewers even if those visitors aren't coming to their site daily.

Making Sales

Companies like Dominos are using chatbot modern technology by permitting customers to make purchases directly with their robots using text message or systems like Facebook Messenger.

This is useful to business like Dominos because it maintains stores from being flooded with numerous phone calls during peak times, and it's helpful to their consumers because it's typically faster and also much less frustrating than calling or making use of the website.

All type of services can take advantage of using a chatbot to assist in making sales, by supplying individualized product suggestion based on input from customers.

Customer care

One of the most typical usages for chatbots is for basic customer service, such as responding to basic concerns, making tips, routing problems to ideal departments, and a lot more.

This is a great for chat robots, because they can programmed with specific actions to your most often asked questions as well as keep you and your staff members from having to field a lot of concerns that could have been addressed by the crawler.

Chatbots can boost customer experience, as well. Customers love getting a solution in seconds without having to wait on hold for an online individual or sending out an email and waiting hours or days for an action.

Studies have revealed that 51% of people believe an organization ought to be available for customer support 24/7. If your business takes 12 hrs to respond to an email, and also your rival addresses an easy inquiry at two o'clock in the morning, whom do you think they will purchase from?

45.8% of individuals would rather call a company with messaging than through email. They recognize email can be slow-moving. They 'd rather utilize an approach that gets much faster, less complicated outcomes.

49.5 would rather speak to a company via messaging than telephone. No person likes waiting on hold, also some people don't like talking on the phone. Messaging is easier for those individuals. The bottom line is that individuals desire chatbots. They conserve them time and also stress, and in return, it conserves you money and time. It's a win-win situation.

Chatbot Solutions

There are currently a variety of chatbot items on the market. Some are fairly efficient, while others have been undoubtedly hurried to market as well as are full of insects that will annoy you and your clients.

Let's take a look at several of the products that are presently on the market and are considered to be top quality.

Botsify

Botsify is another very popular platform that works for Facebook Messenger, however also has a version that functions directly on your web site. They have a totally free strategy (only for Facebook Carrier) that has a great deal of attributes, yet their paid strategies (which can be used on an internet site) begin at a really practical $10 monthly.

Botsify additionally allows human requisition any time, so you can have a customer service agent take control of whenever the chatbot isn't helping the consumer properly.

Chattypeople

The chattypeople system is one of the most prominent chatbots readily available for the Facebook Messenger system, and also works with Facebook remarks.

The chattypeople platform will certainly even permit you to offer items directly to customers via Facebook with Stripe, PayPal, and other settlement systems.

ChitChatChimp

This is at the forefront amongst the chatbots. It enables absolutely any person, even with no programming understanding, to produce their own chatbot.

It can produce all kinds of bots, consisting of:

Customer assistance robots Sales bots Research-gathering bots Educational bots Amusing crawlers.

If you need something versatile as well as customizable that does not cost a fortune, ChitChatChimp is probably your finest alternative.

Conclusion/Outcome

Chatbots can supply real-time interaction that is readily available instantaneously, which is something that also the well-staffed firm is seldom able to do.

While chatbots cannot replace all personnel, they can certainly help you cut down on the variety of times your support staff needs to address basic questions just since customers don't check out the F.A.Q. pages or miss information on sales web pages. They can additionally supply responses from customers that can assist you streamline your, sales and also client service procedures and also make things easier for future customers.

Chapter 4

Voyage of a Digital Traveler

The normal trip of a digital tourist can be divided into five significant phases. As well as artificial intelligence & digitization has currently changed several facets of all those 5 phases considerably. These stages are freely termed as

Dreaming phase,

Preparation stage,

Reserving phase,

Onsite experience phase and also

Comments & experience sharing stage.

I personally think that every traveling plan starts with an amazing dream as well as the resource of that desire could be anything. While browsing so on the net they might find a banner ad at the extreme ideal hand website of an internet page or in an online travel publication. That's primarily an advertisement provided by a traveling business which encourages the user to click on the advertisement, go to their site, choose a travel strategy and after that do the reservations.

Now with the boosting spreading of Artificial Intelligence as well as smart conversational user interfaces, the traveling firms have replaced that banner ad with an Artificial Intelligence Chatbot within that ad unit. This makes it possible for customer to directly speak to the Chatbot and also get concepts about various traveling locations, information referring to set you back and logistics as well as can finally schedule the flight and also hotel tickets in a very all-natural & conversational way. And if you use the Chatbot pair of times for your getaway planning and also reservation, it is smart enough to immediately register your preferences and can straight advise you the appropriate travel plan next time in a really individualized way which suits your requirement. This customization of deals is very crucial today for any type of service due to the fact that according to some studies, about 70% of the customers want individualized as well as tailored information as per his/her preferences and not the common ones.

Traveling sites like Kayak as well as couple of various other sites are giving comparable conversational user interfaces to their clients for preparation and reserving traveling where customer can engage with a Chatbot in natural language either through text or voice and also can do planning and also booking.

Typically individuals invest even more time in planning a holiday journey than the actual trip. Here you can see AI is made use of in many networks where the client is engaged. Many of the prominent travel websites and also mobile applications make use of Chatbot as their interface with the consumers. Networks like Facebook, Slack as well as Skype; traveling websites like booking.com, Sky Scanner have already executed Chatbots in these channels not just for frequently asked questions and questions yet also to aid their consumers for searching, booking and also obtaining assistance on other facets of traveling. There are also various other innovative AI applications that can review your email and calendar as well as recommend you take a trip strategies proactively like traveling site Hipmunk.

Currently let's come to the most interesting stage, the onsite experience stage. There are a couple of travel firms which gives anticipating analytics of various events which might happen and the travels may experience during their travel.

Much of the airlines are additionally now buying anticipating upkeep. So, using equipment knowing as well as other methods like IoT to forecast when an aircraft needs to opt for upkeep. To ensure that it can aid preventing hold-ups and also cancellations because of upkeep related concerns if the very same can be forecasted well in advance.

AI, DL, Augmented Reality, Virtual Reality, and Simulation techniques are now extensively made use of in the Traveling Industry. Most of our digital experiences till currently have actually been experiencing everything and engaging with a screen or a tool from outdoors.

Pre-Travel Experience with Virtual Reality consists of offering an experience of the areas that you are planning to visit and also inspire you to be there. Resort Marriott in United States, using Virtual Reality supplied pre-booking experience to their consumers of visitor locations just to provide the sensation of the location and also influence them to plan a getaway there. Travel businesses are currently embracing this in lots of areas. For instance, Thomas Chef in UK utilizes it for up-selling seats just to give customers pre-booking experiences of distinction of a cheap airfare as well as an economy plus class seat to ensure that client can just experience the distinction of that extra six inches of leg area ahead of time prior to making a booking option.

Quantic airlines has actually carried out Virtual Reality for home entertainment of their extraordinary passenger in the far away flights by providing a new and different experience while they are in a lengthy range tiring as well as tiring trip. It's type of immersing someone right into a totally different experience while in actual he/she is in an entirely various setting or place completely.

AI Facial recognition is also quite interesting modern technology made use of by couple of airlines. Delta for instance has actually leveraged this modern technology for baggage check-in. They make use of the facial recognition to determine the individual and contrast it versus his/her picture in key or driving certificate used throughout the reservation to make certain they are identical. ZetBlue is making use of the similar AI innovation for their guest boarding on to the flight. Dubai airport utilizes identity tunnel to determine the person while he/she is strolling with the passage to the security monitoring. These modern technologies add a lot to minimize the total friction in the traveling.

Now when you get to the destination in your hotel, below likewise AI is used to boost your experience, like determining you automatically in the hotel lobby and also do an automobile check-in right into the hotel. Radisson makes use of a Chatbot for space service.

Currently during your traveling and taking in the sights around the locations, AI made it possible for tools gives you the chance to check out neighborhood areas and the culture. AI applications like Google Translate can assist you equate anything to your own language throughout your traveling.
Coming to traveler security, Simulation techniques are made use of to educate the rescue staffs to provide them an experience really comparable to the real-time scenarios during problems where rescue procedures require to be executed.

The Self-Driving automobile in future most likely to transform the traveling market. Just imagine, a self-driving car and truck getting a consumer from Flight terminal to the hotel or dropping him to a conference. It allows to wait for that day when a self-driving car comes for your pick up at the airport terminal, that's going to be an impressive experience.

The last phase of travel which is your comments after you return from your dream holiday. The comments can be in various kinds like sharing your experience with your close friends as well as family members and motivate them to plan for comparable trips. Some people will certainly share their travel experiences in social media sites by uploading pictures, videos and also remarks. Some people might give their great ranking on the travel site. And someone like me may compose a blog on the outstanding trip they simply had. For a travel company it's very essential to collect such comments as much feasible from their consumers which is most likely to provide valuable info on just how they can improve their solutions additionally and Artificial Intelligence can be of great help here too.

Chapter 5

Super Powerful AI Nations

Russian head of state Vladimir Putin mentioned- AI is the future and also whoever becomes leader in AI will certainly end up being the ruler of the world. Chinese president Xi Jinping stated that China wishes to be the globe leader in AI by 2030. United States White House management voiced - America has been the international leader in AI, and the Trump management will certainly guarantee our great nation remains the worldwide leader in AI. Similarly, National technique for Artificial Intelligence, India released by NITI Aayog indicates its vision as AI-for-All in India. These statements plainly suggest that the race for the superiority in the area of Artificial Intelligence had already taken a great energy as well as AI has taken care of to influence also primary stream national politics as well as the world leaders in a fantastic method.

On the various other hand, several specialists around the world are currently in a large hurry to proclaim which nation is going to be the AI superpower and also that is already in advance in the race. A few of them even persuasively declaring themselves to be an AI superpower simply by building a substitute bubble to draw in the additional interest from the world and some capitalists. Maintaining aside all those concealed programs and prior to also jumping into some conclusion, we need to first take into consideration the requirements to be simple a challenger in this race. Because it's not most likely to be a wholesome competition particularly when we have competitors who are not most likely to shy away from trying any feasible methods whether dishonest or honest to be in advance of the competition. Few of the countries are currently leading in the race, at the very same time there are strong contenders that have big capacity to be in the listing of leaders in the future.

Prior to taking this debate better, we additionally require to define the parameters to determine the supremacy and the variables influencing the exact same. Is it just how much dollar produced utilizing AI by a country or what all core troubles solved for humankind by boosting the top quality of life of the residents of a nation? Additionally, top priorities to be addressed are country and region specific.

As an example, anticipating what film or what advertisement a customer will certainly such as making use of AI may not be something so engaging when it comes to a creating nation like India; rather if AI can deal with some of the core areas like healthcare & medicine, agriculture, food, water, education, urbanization etc. will certainly be much more compelling; and also the success of AI in this instance must be determined in a lot higher terms. To understand this let's take a go back and also talk about the aspects that can basically fuel competitors to be the leaders.

Technically there are 5 major requirements which are important for an AI community to grow in a nation however there might be numerous others that can largely contribute to its advancement and application.

AI Study- AI is basically a developing field and a number of the AI modern technologies are maturing as well as getting far better off with research study, development occurring in regards to the better strategy to take on several of its technical restrictions. There may not had an additional groundbreaking development after the Deep Learning in the last pair of years however there has actually been lots of enhancements and also there were average as well as tiny technologies in terms of just how deep learning and various other AI technologies can be used effectively in several areas; and also all those are essentially because of continual looks into occurring in the area. So, an environment accepting AI research study is very important for a country to progress in the field of AI whether such looks into to be brought out in academic community, within R&D cells of AI companies or in partnership with the government.

Functional Data- Functional information originates from the real-world physical solutions that has been digitized until now, which implies how many physical services has actually been digitized in the nation and also the information from those services has been gathered, stored and made readily available for AI companies, scientists to use for feeding and also enhancing their AI models.

Wealth of AI Engineers and also Information Scientists-
Conventional software designers to come to be AI affluent needs
unique abilities in the areas of device knowing, deep learning, NLP
etc. AI researchers coming from data scientific research background
require even greater abilities and also history to carryout research
study on different locations of AI. Appropriate pool of such AI
designers and also AI researchers are crucial for AI to expand in a
country. The more your Technology institution of higher learning
creating these experienced sources the more your opportunities to
be the leader in the race.

Support from Federal government and also understanding amongst
citizens - Backing from the Federal government and also their
support; might it be developing facilities for AI, framing policies that
sustains AI to expand, encouraging enterprises in adoption of AI or
whatever various other form it could be; the government of a nation
plays a major duty equalizing a climbing modern technology like AI.

Financing and also VC Ecological Community- Appropriate financing
and a fully grown Investor environment is important for AI startups
and also various other AI initiatives in a nation to grow. In some
cases it's not simply funding the AI start-ups but basically leading
them via their journey, counting on and belonging to their vision is

very essential which can just be anticipated from a fully grown VC environment. In spite of having all other AI components a lot of the establishing nations like India and also its young entrepreneurs and also startups are essentially having a hard time in this certain area.

I will attempt to note down few of the leaders and several of the solid challengers right here. The order in which the contenders has actually been noted down in this short article as well as the length of the message created for each has no value on their capabilities and position in the race.

USA undoubtedly is ahead in the race both in terms of AI research study and some of the large range AI implementations. Some of the AI applications previously owned internationally are once again United States products. There is a twist in the tale - unlike other modern technologies, in instance of AI few of the nations are not far behind US and in reality there is an opportunity of leaving behind United States in future.

Canada is well ahead in AI research, it has obtained the finest AI researchers and colleges. Canadian colleges generates several of the very best AI researchers every year. Also talented professionals from all over the world land there to do study on various locations of AI and also convert their concepts into implementable services. Canadian talents are very scholastic and research oriented and there is a real scarcity of real business owners that can take AI beyond the classes and the labs to the roadway. That most likely is the factor, in spite of having most of the talented AI specialists of the globe still they were not been able to create ideal AI products or AI business. Appears Canadian government has currently realized the reality and also currently having significant concentrate on AI application as well as discovering just how to produce income from it. Current imposition of immigration restrictions in the US has actually basically come to be true blessing for Canada and also few various other AI competitors to attract even more as well as much more talents from across the world.

Directly I have got a wonderful regard for China and Chinese entrepreneurs, specifically how it has actually changed itself in past couple of years is incredible as well as we all has an excellent lesson to find out from them. It is not real that you need an excellent out-of-the-box distinct cutting-edge idea or a product to be a successful entrepreneur that several of our young Indian entrepreneurs occasionally mistakenly think. You can basically transform your average concept right into an one-of-a-kind cutting-edge item by including elements like operational excellence, better usability taking right into factor to consider your customer needs; and the very same can come out as an excellent item and that's what happened for several of the Chinese successful items you see today.

20 years ago, China started with what we call a straight imitator as well as they construct reproduction of Google, Amazon, Facebook,

Whatsapp and also so on, the Chinese variation of such items that fits Chinese market as well as Chinese users. Quickly they recognized that if they can provide the very best of the type world class services to their users as well as customers with an addition of local taste on top of it, functions much far better than a common worldwide product. That's most likely one component of the secret dish of China's special form of entrepreneurism.

Visualize you can duplicating a market confirmed product and also you have the capability to do technology on top of it; you will certainly always have a benefit over your competitors. China's formula of worth, entrepreneurism and technology production exists on the reality that there is a massive competition among the Chinese business owners in every domain and also the only way to stand out amongst these rivals is to take your product to a degree at which it is far much better and unmatched. Lots of Chinese business owners has actually already verified their quality in execution, product top quality, speed of bringing products out there as well as much better usage of data in decision making in the company. In regards to excellence in implementation and product quality they have been constantly standing out and also has actually gotten to a stage today which is not just far remarkable to their competitors within and outside China however not replicable and likewise inimitable.

That's the reason Chinese as well as neighboring markets embrace these products. We all recognize that any type of entrepreneurial trip starts with an aggressive implementation and a wonderful vision plan to attain turning points to go after the vision. Yet we frequently forget the truth that execution strategy requires continuous modernization and keeping an eye on to make it appropriate as per the demand of the scenario as well as the dynamics of the marketplace. Chinese entrepreneurs understand how to survive in such extremely competitive environment where the only way of survival is not simply to win however to eliminate all other rivals so that they can't come back again someday.

Additionally, an advantage the Chinese market as well as the Chinese economic climate brings, which again is true even for India is these 2 nations has a substantial domestic test-ground and customer base to attempt as well as test any brand-new idea or any type of item. The fondness of the marketplace is so big that it can take in any type of services or product within that you need not need to even think about any type of other markets a minimum of in the first phases.

An additional reason China leading in AI basically due to the fact that it has actually had the ability to changed itself right into a Cashless, Card-Less, Mobile-Only economic situation. This aided accumulating big useable information which became exceptionally helpful for AI business as well as various other researchers to accelerate their AI growth.

China is concentrating widely on AI Research as well. In the last 3- 4 years the greatest number of AI researcher papers and licenses are been filled by Chinese companies as well as Chinese researchers. The factor China is paving its means towards AI superpower is as a result of the adhering to reasons.

Chinese business along with Chinese Govt. China is the initial really mobile first nation and also Chinese market and Govt. Substantial fund is streaming to Chinese market as well as capitalists are ready to spend on Chinese firms and start-ups.

Protectionist nature of Chinese Govt. offers domestic start-ups a space to settle and also grow to a degree till it ends up being all set to contend with the huge global players in their very early incubation period. Also, Chinese education is more regarding road discovering, practical strategy of discovering and implementing. Chinese government as well as authorities are completely encouraged about the truth that AI is the future as well as therefore constructing their framework to be future AI prepared like a brand-new city is planed near Beijing which is made for self-governing vehicles. It is building a freeways with sensing units for independent lorries as the illumination conditions in the roadway affects the independent automobiles the most which can be confirmed by sensing units along the highways to avoid any kind of mishaps.

It is likewise essential to discuss one significant disadvantage of Chinese AI items that they has not been so effective in broadening beyond China. The language becomes a roadblock for Chinese entrepreneurs when it comes to globalizing their products. So, most likely China is doing excellent in the Chinese market yet not wonderful when it pertains to increasing the business internationally which is really necessary in today's context. Also, Chinese items whatever it could be has a poor online reputation on the quality front.

UK & Europe, Japan, Russia- although having the prospective and also most of the ingredients for AI; have not yet been able to take advantage of those fully to come leading in the list. They have huge functional information yet they have great deals of limitations around it. Despite having some of the great AI researchers and also AI specialists they don't have the kind of solid as well as hardworking entrepreneurs at least in AI room. Japan and Russia- although having great possibilities however requires aggressive execution.

India has a huge number of IT specialists varying from highly experienced to moderate experienced who are currently working with different top worldwide companies and also playing essential roles creating worldwide products or taking care of international procedures. They comprehend such products, they have fair understanding of service designs and also most of them has actually currently delved into the startup world in India developing their own products. A lot of these start-ups are creating AI items in various domain names starting from understood locations like financial & money, medical care, manufacturing, retail etc. to uncommon domains like agriculture, fisheries, marine sources, water management, alternative medications, Ayurveda, security and empowerment of females simply to call a couple of.

AI change in India has already begun in a large means touching throughout nearly all the areas that you can imagine and the world will see the real outcomes of the exact same in coming couple of years.

The National method for Artificial Intelligence, India published by NITI Aayog couple of months back is an exhaustive strategy and also roadmap with a motto of "AI-for-All in India", which reveals exactly how seriously Aayog (payment) as well as Federal government has actually taken AI as well as trying to integrate it with every aspect of our nation as well as its citizens. This is a spots as well as stepping rock for an establishing country's terrific ambition to incorporate modern technology as primary stream in its change journey which I think no country has analyzed it because varied fashion.

This technique clearly reveals exactly how our Aayog as well as our Government has been able to recognize the core locations very certain to Indian conditions where AI can play a vital role and also uplift the economic situation and therefore all various other markets. It has given equivalent significance to the Government, exclusive and public markets while making such method; so you can picture the deepness of thought procedure, know-how, severity and also lot of effort that has went into it to make AI Indianize.

AI is going to bring massive opportunity as well as will certainly boost the Indian economy with an estimated annual growth price of 1.3 percent and in a time of one year an enhancement of extra one trillion USD is just whopping. Based on specialists India supplies the excellent "play ground" for business as well as organizations internationally to develop AI services which can be conveniently carried out in the remainder of the creating and also arising economies and also "Solved in India" objective remains in excellent sync with Artificial Intelligence as a Service (AIaaS).

In health care Tata Memorial Healthcare facility has actually begun functioning on the "Cancer Cells Heat Map" that can lessen with the fostering of AI for India's cancer cells concerns. The Indian government has been making a collection of huge scale treatments to address India's medical care challenges, transformation of 1.5 lakh 'Wellness and also Wellness Centers', developing district healthcare facilities to provide to long-lasting care for non-communicable diseases, 'Ayushman Bharat Goal', promoting e-Health where AI has actually started playing an important function for its success.

In Agriculture, in last couple of years around 50 Indian farming, AI modern technology based start-ups, AgTechs increased more than USD 500 million. Indian startup, Intello Labs, for instance, makes use of image-recognition software application to monitor plants and also predict ranch returns. Aibono makes use of agri-data scientific research and also AI to supply remedies to support crop returns. Trithi Robotics uses drone innovation to permit farmers to keep track of plants in genuine time and supply specific evaluation of their dirt just among others.

In Agriculture, in last couple of years around 50 Indian agricultural, AI modern technology based startups, AgTechs elevated greater than USD 500 million. Indian start-up, Intello Labs, for instance, uses image-recognition software application to keep track of plants as well as predict farm returns. Aibono uses agri-data science and AI to provide services to support crop returns. Trithi Robotics uses drone technology to allow farmers to check plants in actual time and offer exact evaluation of their soil just among others.

Also, remedies like plant health tracking as well as giving live activity advisories to farmers and utilizing picture classification devices incorporated with regional as well as remote noticed data bringing an innovative adjustment in utilization as well as performance of farm equipment in Indian farming. AI powered applications for Dirt Treatment, AI app for Sowing, App for Herbicide Optimization and AI app for Accuracy Farming have been executed in several states in India.

In Education and learning, Indian startups along with Central and also State federal governments has actually already changed country and also various other education and learning systems making use of flexible understanding tools for tailored learning and intelligent and also interactive tutoring systems. An example, Andhra Pradesh federal government is predicting School Dropouts making use of AI and taking actions to decrease it. AI tools has actually been made use of to automated rationalization of teachers and also advancement of customized expert training courses for identification and also fulfillment of understanding as well as ability spaces by number of state federal governments and various other academic bodies.

In the location of Smart Cities as well as Smart Leaving, a substantial financial investment has been started for developing Smart Parks & public centers, Smart Residences, AI driven solution shipment (such as anticipating solution shipment on the basis of resident data, justification of administrative personnel on the basis of forecasted service need as well as migration pattern analysis, and AI based grievance redressal with chat-bots and wise assistants), Group management, Smart safety systems, protecting against cyber-attacks as well as much more.

In Transportation as well as Smart Wheelchair India Federal government has great focus on application of Artificial Intelligence to attend to concerns connected to Flexibility and also Transportation, specifically challenges we came across in India daily.
Several of the tough locations discussed are Congestion as well as road crashes, High variety of traffic fatalities, Absence of public transport facilities etc

. AI aided smart modern technologies like Assisted Lorry, Greenfield Infrastructure, Autonomous Trucking, Intelligent Transportation Equipments, Traveling Course & Flow Optimization and also Area Based Car park will be utilized to attend to a lot of these tough areas. Yet the most important areas which will certainly take India ahead front in AI race is the 'National AI Marketplace (NAIM)' and 'Information Market'. Some preliminary effort on these 2 areas has currently been begun yet the day these two campaigns comes to a good condition, nobody can quit India to be top in the list of AI Superpowers.

A number of the recent happenings in India on AI front brought about by Indian start-ups in cooperation with Technology Giants and in organization with leading Technology Institutes and the federal government has not obtained that media hype internationally however trust me, there are several fantastic points has actually begun taking place in this country as well as the whole globe will see the outcomes in coming couple of years.

Although recently but the entrepreneurial attitude of young generation in India has actually already set to fire. The danger taking capabilities, the need to do something brand-new, the concern to do something for nation as well as the country males, to reveal the world that "It can quite take place in India" attitude of our brand-new generation is becoming a true blessing for the technical transformation in India.

Any type of technological training be it AI is conveniently accessible and also extremely economical in India. India in truth has a conductive atmosphere for AI to prosper better than any kind of various other country of the world. India is currently an IT powerhouse and also in various other words an IT Superpower and also it has got significant capacity to come leading in the race of AI Superpowers.

Chapter 6

Self Driving Cars

The most generally asked inquiries regarding independent cars are discussed and I've dived deeper into each of those here.

Degree by degree or straight to level five?
The significant presumption is that "Everything that moves will go self-governing", and also we are not just speaking regarding vehicles, all the vehicles on our roadways, drones in the skies, purchasing automobiles and also toys will relocate on its own to the degree that our involvement will certainly come to be rudimentary, undesired or perhaps prohibited.

Just how will we obtain there?

There is a six-level categorization scheme that comes from Culture of Automotive Engineers & additionally describes the automated driving in a six groups.

Degree Absolutely No: Motorist Just
This one is easy, it's when you totally drive on your own.

Level One: Assisted

Vehicles that we mainly drive today belong here, those are the ones that have anti-lock brakes as well as cruise-control, so they can take control of some non-vital procedures associated with driving.

Degree Two: Partial Automation

When the system can take over control in some certain usage situations yet driver still has to check system constantly is below, it applies to circumstances when the vehicle is self-driving the freeway as well as you simply sit there and expect it to behave well.

Level 3: Conditional Automation

This level indicates that chauffeur doesn't have to check the system all the time yet has to remain in a setting where the control can swiftly be returned to by a human driver. That suggests no requirement to have hands on a guiding wheel yet you have to leap in at the audios of the emergency scenario, which system can identify effectively.

Level 4: High Automation

When your automobile drives you to the parking area you obtain to the degree four, when there is no requirement for a human operator for a particular use situation or a part of a trip.

Degree 5: Full Automation

The divine grail exists here as well as suggests that the system can manage all the circumstances instantly throughout the entire trip as well as no chauffeur is called for to the factor of not having controls at all, which means you have no option.

What kind of sensors? LIDAR or otherwise?

The following concern is which hardware will permit us to get to the degree 5, whether it's got to be some incremental improvements or brand-new sensing units to the current ones?

Business like Google are relying upon LIDAR technology, which stands for Light Discovery and also Ranging and is a remote picking up method that utilizes light in the form of a pulsed laser to measure ranges (variable ranges) to the surrounding atmosphere.

That 3D laser map incorporated with video cameras as well as clever software program, is adequate details for an automobile to drive itself on a road without a human driver.

The current implementation is a relocating container on a roof that sets you back $78000, which makes it a significant challenge from being used throughout the sector on a range. Yet there are some advances to make it strong state without relocating parts which would certainly cost around $260.

What concerning stereo electronic cameras that permit us to compute 3D area? The kind of cameras human beings have in their eyes that permit us not to encounter each various other. These cameras obtain us nearly all benefits of LIDAR and also do not set you back that a lot, yet the counter debate is additional resolution as well as precision.

Brand-new sorts of pre-computed maps?
Everybody makes use of Google Maps, Waze, Apple Maps as well as they have an amazing level of resolution that make our movement throughout the city frictionless. This resolution is still not sufficient for a vehicle which wants to drive on its own.

What information is missing? Points like:
where are the contours
where are the website traffic barrels
what time of the day do I obtain a glare in front of my video camera that blinds me entirely

And also all other sort of mini resolution details are entirely missed out from the generalized view of maps. Since we as humans uncommitted about that whatsoever and also those existing maps services are for people, not machines.

So do we require to different pre-computed maps just for

independent vehicles? It looks like yes, but that is most likely to provide them and just how much will that cost? And also one of the most interesting concern that is nobody asking, if there is an opportunity for a monopoly in this room? Due to the fact that in the closest future when we reach the level five as well as you are entrusted no selection of running the vehicle on your own- you are completely dependent on the framework that powers the self-driving car.

Will we see the less expensive variation of pre-computed maps that will allow our vehicles to run within a certain reduced rate or with a certain degree of safety and security?

Who will manage this possible hazardous grey area?

It additionally has power implications, given that you have to depend on a supercomputer in your trunk to operate those complicated multimillion criterion pre-computed HD maps, and also kid those will certainly drain a whole lot of power.

What mix of software techniques?
Deep Learning is making a noise across the Silicon Valley yet there are other achievements in the field of robotics and also course finding that need to not be failed to remember. The significant difference between those approaches is the ability of a system to

gain from a previous experience/dataset or drive decision solely based upon a hardwired logic or regulations.

As a matter of reality the Boston Dynamics robotics that we all appreciate don't take advantage of any kind of machine learning in any way, while still providing outstanding outcomes.

Although those directly programmed rules cannot beat Alpha-Go players with the very same level of performance as Deep Learning algorithms they can still be combined with the current advances in machine learning to provide far better outcomes.

Will V2X radios play a vital function?
V2X is a form of modern technology that enables lorries to communicate with relocating parts of the website traffic system around them. And V2V modern technology, or automobile to automobile, allows cars to interact with other lorries.

The use cases range from having your auto communicating with a website traffic light when there are nothing else cars as well as you are resting there for 5 mins to more dangerous scenarios where automobiles need to urgently communicate the state of emergency such as a T-bone collision issue.

Which is specifically interesting taking into consideration current advancements of Tesla as well as a viral video clip of an automobile identifying the collision mishap means prior to a human could.

If proper interaction existed on the roadway and also around it, envision how several accidents can be prevented.

The major worry below is a protocol compatibility as well as efficiency of interaction considering that the decision ought to occur in nanoseconds and there is no time at all for additional computation associated to distinctions in a communication "language".

This is an innovation everyone sees as terrific future, but no one prepares for it as a very first iteration of totally independent lorries.

Just how will automakers "localize" their vehicles?

Every city has various driving culture, so how will independent vehicles deal with these special conditions. What's secure in Bangalore may trigger a website traffic collapse in Boston, etc

Localization is a term originating from computer system scientific research and also indicates that software program will certainly somehow be prepared to the conditions of setting where it is carried out.

So which kind can this take in self-driving cars and trucks, will we have different sort of algorithms devoted to various cities? Boston version, Bangalore variation etc for each city driving conventions? Or will we have a generalized algorithm that is able to adapt to any type of setting by investing a long time on a road?

This associates with a whole various other area of research study that includes producing learning policies by soaking up how individuals and objects around us behave. By finding out social conventions and regular human behavior autos should have the ability to perform better.

Exactly How Will Crash Fees Change?
If all cars and trucks end up being autonomous the accident prices will certainly be absolutely no given that the majority of, 24 of 25 reasons for accidents are human error relevant. Points like speeding, sidetracked driving, driving under the influence, running red lights are all reasons for us resting behind the wheel.

But what regarding the combined state of things? Where some cars and trucks will be still driven by human beings and will certainly cause unanticipated crashes that we have actually never experienced prior to.
When will it end up being prohibited to drive?
If it holds true that algorithms are statistically better than vehicle drivers then we shouldn't let individuals to drive. There are still a

whole lot of individuals that love to drive. This can be an enjoyable entertainment activity however we just do not require those people on the roadway.

There are a variety of predictions by significant gamers that specify this will happen by 2025-2035. If we are prepared sufficiently, we will certainly see this attractive globe throughout the life time.

Chapter 7

AI in BFSI

As we are heading towards a revolutionary change from an age of digitization to an era of cognification, we need to confess that our banks and financial organizations worldwide are the ones who has actually identified the possibilities of Artificial Intelligence at an extremely onset and also embraced it in their transformation journey. Utilizing Artificial Intelligence to redefine their products, processes as well as the strategies is the major factor to consider for the majority of the center financial institutions and also banks today.

There are many areas of Financial Industry where Artificial Intelligence as well as Device Learning has already developed it's impact yet there are still lots of areas that are untouched and are most likely to be the core focus in the coming years.

The monetary services industry can be broadly identified right into 3 significant segments where AI has actually ended up being the need-of-the-day today. They are Capital Market, Customer Banking as well as Insurance policy which almost covers the majority of the sector.

Robo Advisors, High Frequency Trading, Risk Management, Anti-

Money Laundering, Cyber Protection, Scams Detection, Intelligent Suggestions and also forecasts are couple of areas where AI applications has actually always been linked to. In fact there are numerous even more areas in financial sector where AI has currently been playing a crucial function that many of us most likely not much mindful of those.

Artificial Intelligence has the ability to procedure substantial quantity of information extremely promptly which is much more data than since has actually been refined in the past by human or any type of traditional computer system programs. As well as that's going to improve the banks to give far better solutions that they give to their consumers. In wide range monitoring they will certainly have the ability to supply far better, extra targeted and also reliable suggestions to their clients.

Danger and also Credit Scores Assessment is an area where Artificial intelligence and Deep Learning are playing the function of a video game changer and insurance coverage market has adopted it greatly. They are finding it very engaging largely due to the fact that AI is to just altering their business totally.

Smart pocketbook is going to be an additional area of passion for the financial institutions around the world, the banks will certainly give smart budgets to its consumers, AI made it possible for wise pocketbooks will look at consumer's investing routines and it will pick up from his/her habits to give clever encourages and referrals of future spending. It will encourage financial savings and also accountable spending on their credit score & debit cards in the form of predictive signals and referrals. AI can find if a consumer is likely to change their solutions or products, this very early signal will assist banks to offer him/her extra suitable item which may assist keeping the customer.

Currently concerning the Risk Evaluation, Credit Report evaluation and Regulative areas, today if you desire to get a financing, in a traditional method a house lending or an individual financing takes number of weeks' time or might be even a lot more to get rid of all kinds of credit rating checks prior to approving such fundings. With Artificial Intelligence the processing preparation will boil down to a hr or max 2. Because AI's capability to do credit analysis in much faster as well as far better way by interrogating numerous customer data resources, this is.

We are already experiencing the modification in the interface the financial institutions having with their customers. They are significantly altering those to Chatbots, Robots and also Humanoids as their initial line of user interfaces with their customers to boost solution experiences. We are seeing the comparable trends in the Financial institutions in India also.

ICICI bank has actually leveraged AI for face and voice acknowledgment in few of its items. HDFC Bank, Yes Financial Institution, Axis Bank, DBS Financial Institution, and also few others are all set with their AI powered Chatbots and also Virtual Assistance user interfaces.

Likewise there are great deals of AI applications turning up right into locations like Anti-Money Laundering and Regulations because it's extremely simple for an AI system to evaluations great deal of information at its finger pointers as well as determine the patterns and also better determine fraudulent, cash laundering as well as criminal tasks swiftly and highlight those to the bank authorities well ahead of time to make sure that instant actions can be required to jail those tasks.

Other locations of AI booming in the economic sector are utilizing facial anxiety evaluation to immediately detect ATM frauds. AI monetary advisers called Robo Advisers work proactively for its clients providing knowledge 24x7.

Chapter 8

AI and Social Media

The Way Open AI released the outcomes of their recent study was implied to freak us out, and also it functioned. The A.I. Text Generator That's too dangerous to reveal gives examples where with really little input, text is produced that is indistinguishable otherwise much better than the high quality of this writing.
The code had not been released for others to construct and also check upon, yet it's likely that similar versions will remain in various other's hands quickly.

Automated Messages are involving social media, and also if social media sites is to survive, it definitely will not be in its existing kind. There's a saying, always bank on text as the finest medium for social communication. And also lots of have. Social media, social media sites, Amazon.com as well as Yelp testimonials,
and numerous other tools use text as core to their worth. What happens when the cost to generate a message that appears authentic falls to zero?

All wagers are off.

Italian philosopher and also researcher at CNRS Gloria Orrigi observes because info intends to be therefore plentiful and also cost-free, we are shifting our connection to expertise to depend on reputation:

We are experiencing a basic paradigm shift in our partnership to knowledge. From the 'details age', we are moving towards the 'credibility age', in which information will certainly have value just if it is already filtering system, assessed as well as commented upon by others. Seen in this light, online reputation has actually come to be a main column of cumulative knowledge today. It is the gatekeeper to understanding, and also the keys to the entrance are held by others. The method which the authority of expertise is currently created makes us reliant on what are the unavoidably biased judgments of various other individuals, many of whom we do not know. She suggests a secret is assisting individuals discern the reputational paths.

What a fully grown resident of the electronic age ought to be proficient at is not detecting and confirming the honesty of the information. Instead, she should be qualified at rebuilding the reputational course of the piece of information in inquiry, evaluating the purposes of those who flowed it, and also figuring out the schedules of those authorities that leant it trustworthiness.

We have actually recognized the demand for social media

proficiency given that it started. Howard Rheingold's research study and publication Net Smart steams it down to Five Literacies: attention,

involvement, cooperation, essential consumption of information (or "crap discovery"), and also network smarts. The issue is literacy does not disperse generally.

And also what Hemingway called Crap Discovery is concerning to become extremely hard, if not costly.

In the early days of social networks and social media we had Bots & Fakesters, often for enjoyable. When Friendster prohibited Fakesters till they might, back monetize them, Tribe.net welcomed them, genuine identity was lost as a prospective social media sites primitive. Fakesters became a function, not an insect.

And also you might inform when content was being immediately generated. The firehose of fake would overwhelm the feed. And as business as well as political interests started to dip into the liquidity of attention, astroturfing was quickly discernible. Like with spam, the assaults became a lot more sophisticated, as well as social platforms connection to Fakesters and great intents not to censor caused halfhearted countermeasures. The platforms assumed neutral positions as typical providers up until the Russians woke us up.

This was also when it was identified that web content was the challenge drive social media network development. The socials media became much less conversational, from what are you doing? to what's taking place? on Twitter as a point.

The move to web content brought with it raised personalization, and also recommendations, including dreadful instances such as when formulas believe you wish to die.
The platforms have some major modifications to make for exactly how they target as well as filter, and also some have made admirable moves.

With web content came its typical proprietors, which gained the DMCA Takedown Notification weapon for which systems always promptly comply.

The whole situation appears unimportant as well as absurd, but actually tells us quite a whole lot about how the net functions and the methods in which individuals weaponize copyright regulation to censor, hide things they would certainly prefer were forgotten, or threaten others.

I'm sharing this unusual example to highlight that regulations will not equal this adjustment either. This year in the US we'll possibly obtain some great personal privacy protection (someplace in between the

EU and California) for our information. That might in-part safeguard us against the 3rd party targeting of automated messages.

Hyper-targeting is a tool of the last war, and automated messages might imply a brand-new front. If you can target somebody without a robust behavioral, what profile, as well as rather simply counter-message. In a few years we'll all have our very own individual giants, equipped with automated messages. Talking with us in detail authentically, at first operator-assisted, and also quickly the input of our questions and point of views will be enough.

That targeting, btw, doesn't require the genuine identity social networks don't have anyhow (conserve, LinkedIn). There are regulations to great astroturfers, however in no-way can enforcement stay on top of the assault, that may also be an excellent point if you count on the 1st Modification.

In this afraid new world, the counter-measure might be giving people the devices to defend themselves. Platforms that supply the course for automated messages need to be in charge of revealing their reputational courses. And perhaps Open.ai ought to launch the designs so toolmakers can encourage individuals to create their very own automated messages. So you can respond to your individualized giants directly with the exact same comfort they have.

Chapter 9

Ethics in AI

Artificial intelligence (AI) as well as machine learning are revolutionizing markets and societies at huge. Their capabilities are embedded in our everyday lives and also their applications are expanding. The outcomes of their decisions currently affect lives, and also with that comes considerable danger. For these innovations to remain to have a favorable effect on culture, they need to follow by mankind's values and principles. Technology is just as good as its maker, so everybody operating in the area is in charge of producing a moral framework for AI that reflects our worth. This starts by looking inwards and reviewing our own beliefs.

From a young age, individuals, society, education, faith, politics as well as media shape our overview and also beliefs concerning the globe. These experiences generate info that our minds categorize and link to understand all of it. These groups often create stereotypes, which set off cognitive associations about characteristics like sex, age as well as race that don't reflect fact. This has harmful influence on culture. The problem is this process is immediate, automated and typically not something we understand is occurring. The majority of would certainly contradict a discriminatory thought that slides right into awareness, but given that behavior is mainly identified by the unconscious mind, favorable intentions are inadequate.

To make sure that AI does no injury, we must proceed with care. We require to shield our honest standards and incorporate them into a framework that overviews the design, implementation and energy of AI in culture.

... offered that practices is greatly determined by the unconscious mind, favorable intentions are not nearly enough.

Honest Framework

The thorough record called Fairly Aligned Style was created to notify, upskill and also assistance organizations that produce AI of the significance of values in modern technologies that encourage humanity. Created by thousands of diverse idea leaders throughout various techniques, the file lays out some crucial moral concepts that AI decision-making must follow.

Each of these principles are essential to a genuinely "moral AI", and also this write-up suggests that the concepts remain in reality reliant and also interconnected on 3 more comprehensive Concepts:

Intelligibility: The technological processes are transparent as well as explainable.

Precision: The level to which the result is agent of the fact.

Fairness: The decision-making is objective and made regardless of sensitive data.

Coined by the UK government, 'intelligibility' of AI produces liability for the end results of their decisions. If they are being made use of and also consequently whether human legal rights have been infringed, expertise of just how as well as why decisions are made enables customers to understand. Lifting the cover on opaque systems is necessary to develop the accuracy of its computational techniques, and also just with precise insight can society start to trust its area in the decision-making process. Comprehending the precision of understandings and their influence on civil rights is critical to making certain that the results are reasonable and also promote positive health.

1. Intelligibility

Today's formulas decide a whole lot of points concerning us- who gets employed, that gets discharged, who obtains a home loan and also that is an unsafe wrongdoer- which can make what might be a challenging choice, basic. A number of high-profile instances have actually questioned the validity of the black box choices, which fired up the need for 'apprehensible' AI systems- those that are explainable as well as technically clear.

" When algorithms influence civil rights, public values or public decision-making, we need oversight as well as transparency"-

Marietje Schaake, Participant of the European Parliament.

Raising the cover on black box systems is essential to examine and scrutinize the legitimacy of AI's result, however the intricacy of the multi-layered semantic networks creates very hard auditing. The gravity of these choices on individuals' lives, however, demands that artificial intelligence structures be explainable from input to outcome, which is a huge element to begin thinking concerning from the design phase. The Department of Protection said that the inability to explain the inner workings of AI systems limits their effectiveness. To battle these limitations they are presently creating the Explainable AI Program (XAI). Its goal is to create maker discovering methods that can clarify their approach whilst preserving their predictive power as well as the copyright of the code.

XAI Idea

" When people fly in an aircraft, they do not need to understand precisely how the plane works to feel safe flying. They simply need to recognize that the plane abides by certain air travel safety guidelines". paraphrasing an interesting comparative instance I listened to in a talk just recently from Ivana Bartoletti, Head of Personal Privacy and also Data Security at Gemserv as well as Co-Founder of Female Leading in AI Network.

You must not have to be a data scientist to recognize an AI's reasoning. This info needs to be available and also readily available in different forms to every kind of user, from academics to the basic population. When customers can understand just how as well as why outcomes are produced, they can more conveniently trust its accuracy and also fairness.

Not all services have to be technological. Regulations like GDPR have actually also brought in a number of stipulations about automated decision-making with no human involvement, consisting of the requirement to reveal when and just how this procedure is used. Organizations have to provide accessibility to the information, the logic/rules and also the audit trail for any automated AI decisions, in addition to making the customer familiar with that decided-equipment or human. The age of unaccountable equipments is therefore over. The concern of liability has been moved to the makers of AI to make certain that developments in innovation do not come with the price of human principles and values.

2. Precision

AI and device learning have actually revolutionized the rate, efficiency as well as cost of crunching big quantities of data. The powers and also capabilities of the innovations have done every little thing from surpassing physicians at recognizing lung cancer kinds and also heart condition, creating sci-fi movies as well as also defeating 2 of Risk's best candidates. AI has likewise got it dramatically wrong.

The objective of AI as well as maker understanding is to aid humanity, not change it. Until absolutely unmistakable AI systems are achieved, their outputs ought to just be made use of to help with discussion whilst professionals continue to be the last decision maker.

While managing the role of AI in decision-making, we must additionally be checking out as well as checking their outcomes. Organizations seldom identify the value of good top quality input data until the AI is already in public usage.

The goal of AI as well as artificial intelligence is to aid humanity, not change it.

Recognizing unpredictability makes it possible to make rational decisions based on the risks of wrong decisions. The opportunity to make equipment learning mindful and also vital of data as well as its very own decision-making is as a result possible, yet the problem of responsibility is still on engineers to implement these strategies proactively. Accuracy is frequently judged ad-hoc as soon as the AI is currently in human usage, but the severe effect of inaccurate choices on human life and also values requires that these methods be incorporated in the style phase before real-life application.

Bayesian inference

AI as well as machine learning have actually enabled us to create insights better of precision than ever, yet human beings must not be totally eliminated from the decision-making loophole. In the period of phony news and also misinformation, it's important that clinical rigour remains to be at the heart of discovery while we proceed to construct on the body of realities and truth. Just with extensive screening and placing accuracy at the core of the layout concepts will certainly people trust AI, which is important to the acceptance of its energy and insights in society.

3. Fairness

Exact understandings are critical to reasonable decision-making. There is much debate around what is truly 'fair' choice making, yet in other words, it is the equal, unbiased treatment of all groups/variables in a choice without impact from qualities such as gender, race or religious beliefs. Real fairness starts with information that represents a wide range of attributes, importance, ideas and ideas, which affects exactly how algorithms are trained as well as subsequently just how machine learning models choose. Algorithms as well as the information made use of to educate them are generated by individuals as well as people are unavoidably and inherently prejudiced. Microsoft learnt by hand when they launched a crawler on Twitter called Tay, who came to be a racist, sexist, anti-sematic tyrant requesting all feminists to "burn in heck". The bot itself was unbiased, yet the training information created by Twitter individuals was not.

Along with biased training data, behind every algorithm is a private with individual beliefs that develop the basis of how machine learning decisions are made, referred to as 'mathematical prejudice'. The try out Tay was an unfavorable knowing curve for Microsoft without severe implications various other than poor publicity, however mathematical predisposition in other situations has caused unethical, unjust therapy.

Algorithms and the information used to train them are generated by people and individuals are unavoidably as well as inherently biased. The formulas used to evaluate the training data did not change for these predispositions and also included their very own prejudices that bolstered these stereotypes. As exemplified by the current conflicts with face acknowledgment software program, a prejudiced training information establish effects just how well innovation can take care of diverse data and individuals, which subsequently restricts their capability to react fairly and also objectively.

MIT Media Lab researcher Pleasure Buolamwini demonstrating just how AI face recognition functions substantially better for white faces than black faces.
The datasets utilized to train machines must be carefully curated to show varied features, cultures, values and also beliefs such that any choice made is rep of the whole population, not simply an option of it. The trouble is that information is 'identified' from previous

decision-making, which frequently mirrors undesirable bias and underrepresentation of minorities. Consequently, AI can learn to mirror the predispositions as well as reflect that in its very own decision-making, thus bolstering and reproducing the historic predispositions.

'feature design' in machine learning, which entails data makeover to promote modeling, stresses specific attributes as well as variables over others. The variables it is programmed to focus on have a substantial impact on the classifications, distinctions and information made downstream in the machine learning process. This risks getting rid of vital yet nuanced attributes and distinctions from the final decision if teams are over-simplified or wrongly classified.

The applications of AI as well as machine learning have expanded to settings which have to follow by a collection of honest and also social norms that differ in between professions, cultures as well as nations. An AI applied in a medical setup sticks to various moral standards to in an insurance setting- gender can determine your vehicle insurance coverage price but not your access to clinical treatment- however instructing AI how to act in every feasible scenario is very intricate as well as always transforming as values advance.

Until AI itself can be made genuinely fair, the machine learning process should be moderated and also corrected for its fairness from beginning to end up in a traceable and clear means. Open source tools like IBM's AI Fairness 360 can help attain this, but GDPR makes accessibility to this information difficult and also typically difficult, so organizations need to learn just how to recognize prejudice in their information without awareness of the secured features affixed to it.

AI Justness 360 trial

Variety has long been considered as the trick to innovation and monetary success, however it is also required for creating and regulating 'reasonable' AI systems. A diverse series of backgrounds will naturally create a wide variety of viewpoints, clarified concealed biases and also supply much deeper, more imaginative insight right into how to eliminate predisposition from the process. The group must also originate from a series of techniques, including ethicists, psycho therapists and also sociologists, to value the social and cultural context that AI runs in.

Those influenced by mathematical decision-making can also take part in promoting justness via a procedure that allows them to report discriminatory AI-made decisions. In America, instructors had their benefits, pay increases and employment statuses made a decision by a mathematical 'Worth Added Version', which was extensively rescinded after repeated complaints of transparency, accuracy and justness of its decisions. By working to ensure that the recipients of AI decision-making, no issue their history, are dealt with fairly as people as well as equals, AI can offer to shield and also improve social and also individual health.

Final Thoughts

For AI and also machine learning to have a lasting, positive influence on humanity, they should be guided by the very same honest precepts and concepts that humans themselves abide by. The expanding contexts that AI and also machine learning are being used in means that they need to abide by collections of facility, value-laden concepts.

Just through intelligibility, fairness and accuracy can humankind leverage the power and alleviate the risks that AI and machine learning continue to develop- technological financial obligation in AI must not bring about honest financial obligation in society.

Chapter 10

Automation and Jobs

Automation is progressively proliferating nearly every facet of our lives and almost every market. Whether it is banking and finance, vehicle, production, aviation, consumer service, medicine & medical care, it's everywhere and also almost daily automation is entering an increasing number of new fields. Some specialists and also financial experts already forecasted that there's most likely to be some level of joblessness in numerous industries due to Automation as well as Artificial Intelligence which they describe as "Technological Joblessness".

One of the most essential concern that emerges today while a company planning to introduce any kind of modern automation methods is exactly how the workers affected will react to it? Will they develop a compatibility with those little automation programs or they will start seeing them as a competition? Believe me, every administration has actually gone via this sensitive element while pondering an automation campaign in their companies.

The excellent information is, if we look back in the history, many of the fantastic creations occurred in last 200 years have actually been developed to replace human labor. As well as in various celebrations, the financial experts, professionals & scholars have

actually elevated an alarm informing "We will certainly be lacking jobs and also we are making our skills out-of-date".
But fortunately, every time those alarms have actually become incorrect in the past.

For an instance, when the Automated Teller Machine (ATM) was presented to automate the standard and also routine banking functions, it did not destroy the role of a Bank employee; rather banks operated more effectively and Human bank employee function moved to do even more complex jobs. As a result allowing financial institutions to open an increasing number of branches than it had been prior to causing a general rise in the quantity of banking jobs.

As per a record published by Globe Bank, estimates around 66% of Indian service industry tasks are at risk because of automation. And also India isn't alone, in China it would certainly be around 75% as well as in a similar way other countries. In Indian IT Solution Market alone, about 6.5 lakhs low-skilled placements are in danger.

These professionals also forecasted that the new wave of modern-day automation is "Blind to the Color of your Collar". That indicates it's going to influence both Blue as well as White Collar work. A growing number of regular workplace tasks like customer assistance as well as clerical work will certainly be affected the most, however also other semi-skilled and also proficient tasks are also not totally safe.

Let's assess why this time it's various than the previous false alarms.

Industrial transformation has offered the "Mechanical Power" to the machines, the power to do recurring points in much bigger range, faster as well as with much more efficiently than a normal human can do. IT change in 80's and 90's has actually provided "Computational Capability" to the devices, ability to procedure repeated computational jobs in much faster and reliable means. This time, Artificial Intelligence has offered the "Cognitive Capacity" to the devices. Cognitive skills include, capability to find out, examine, factor and apply those understandings. Tools and also equipments we are utilizing are becoming a lot more and also much more intelligent. Is it going to be a genuine risk for our work?

One more group of professionals has some different point of view, they argue that in the future automation in fact develops more work than what it eliminates. Makers are best at completing repeated tasks as well as raise general performance which frees up great deal of time for the workers to concentrate on "Intellectually Testing" as well as "Creative Works". And automation as well as Artificial Intelligence will basically match human skills and also abilities as opposed to totally replacing them. They likewise believe that it's most likely to be a period of "Male & Machine Partnership". Artificial Intelligence will certainly get rid of or reduce tasks which are repetitive in nature as well as less intellectually difficult however new forms of work will certainly take their location.

Automation is not about altogether replacing the human element, yet concerning raising the duty people play and the worth they bring to their work roles. While there are some critical challenges that automation might bring with itself, it has actually become a necessity for virtually all organizations today and we need to also take into consideration the merits it will certainly have on the organization.

Chapter 11

Jobs and AI

The major worry below is a protocol compatibility as well as efficiency of interaction considering that the decision ought to occur in nanoseconds and there is no time at all for additional computation associated to distinctions in a communication "language".

This is an innovation everyone sees as terrific future, but no one prepares for it as a very first iteration of totally independent lorries.

Can we get rid of traffic signal?
Four-way lights draw and also if the autos can speak to each various other and are completely autonomous why cannot we do away with lights. This may seem extremely chaotic initially however hey, aren't internet packets relocating the very same means?

This would certainly include having smart rearranging formulas and also extreme monitoring at a factor of junctions but this is absolutely worth it, taking into consideration the renovations it will bring to the efficiency of transport.

Just how will automakers "localize" their vehicles?

Every city has various driving culture, so how will independent vehicles deal with these special conditions. What's secure in Bangalore may trigger a website traffic collapse in Boston, etc

. Localization is a term originates from computer system scientific research and also indicates that software program will certainly somehow be prepared to the conditions of setting where it is carried out.

So which kind can this take in self-driving cars and trucks, will we have different sort of algorithms devoted to various cities? Boston version, Bangalore variation etc for each city driving conventions? Or will we have a generalized algorithm that is able to adapt to any type of setting by investing a long time on a road?

This associates with a whole various other area of research study that includes producing learning policies by soaking up how individuals and objects around us behave. By finding out social conventions and regular human behavior autos should have the ability to perform better.

That will win? Silicon Valley vs China vs Incumbents

The significant presumption below is that incumbents are the ones that have the easiest method to success given that they are currently making automobiles as well as have actually all the needed framework.

These business are establishing workplaces in Silicon Valley and aggressively trying to employ people to drive the advancement faster because they comprehend this is going to occur via software mostly. There is also a chance for an indigenous Silicon Valley cars and truck company, like Tesla.

And also there are plenty of Chinese manufacturers as well as software application proprietors like Baidu that are really boldly pressing in the direction of this space. On a side note China publishes much more documents on deep learning than any type of other nation on earth, so absolutely worth watching on.

Will we buy automobiles or transportation as a solution?
If we as consumers will certainly alter our behavior from acquiring cars and trucks from manufacturers to acquiring transportation solution from companies like Uber and Lyft, the entire lots of loan will certainly start floating to the another direction.

This will certainly cause the car market to look more like an airline company market, where you do not necessarily select which plane you would such as to fly on yet dedicate your cash to a fleet supplier-airline business.

This will create auto business to change right into b2b companies as opposed to B2C as well as they will certainly begin offering to fleet supervisors like Uber. Therefore, we won't see any kind of Super Bowl advertisements for autos and many various other points that exist to manipulate us right into buying automobiles will go vanished.

Exactly How Will Insurance Modification?
And among such changes will be the insurance policy sector. Today insurance policy costs are calculated as a feature that takes you as a driver, your demographics, expense of the automobile that you have as well as where you live.
What will insurer take into consideration the components within this new self-driving age? Will the effectiveness of an algorithm be the core metrics? Automobile manager? Auto supplier? Or still a chauffeur that rents an automobile or owns?

Just how will the repair work costs behave? We will certainly have less accidents on a range but how challenging will be the actual repair work of your laser systems, pre-computed map supercomputer analyzers and all other costly equipment.

Exactly How Will Crash Fees Change?
If all cars and trucks end up being autonomous the accident prices will certainly be absolutely no given that the majority of, 24 of 25 reasons for accidents are human error relevant. Points like speeding,

sidetracked driving, driving under the influence, running red lights are all reasons for us resting behind the wheel.

But what regarding the combined state of things? Where some cars and trucks will be still driven by human beings and will certainly cause unanticipated crashes that we have actually never experienced prior to.

When will it end up being prohibited to drive?
If it holds true that algorithms are statistically better than vehicle drivers then we shouldn't let individuals to drive. There are still a whole lot of individuals that love to drive. This can be an enjoyable entertainment activity however we just do not require those people on the roadway.

Just how will commutes transform?
One argument is that commute times will take longer due to the fact that we will certainly become indifferent to just how long the commute will take. As we approach the state where all cars and trucks are completely self-governing, there are no traffic signal and there are no crashes, we need to have the ability to do anything we desire during the commute.

Heck, we can even rest during the commute like we do on planes or trains. Commute will definitely change from something agonizing to a much nicer task.

Likewise this will certainly release up so much area (car park spots, car repair work stores) that people will live a lot closer to the job and also won't have to commute as much as today.

Just how will cities change?

There are many second and also 3rd order impacts that will certainly take place and also that are difficult to anticipate right currently, as it was difficult to anticipate the phenomenon of Walmart.
These things will most definitely transform our culture and develop hidden opportunities to exploit on.

When Will This Start and after that just how rapidly will we change to independent autos?

There are a variety of predictions by significant gamers that specify this will happen by 2020- 2040. If we are prepared sufficient, we will certainly see this attractive globe throughout the life time as well as the question is.

Chapter 12

Jobs Immune to AI and Automation

With the increase of artificial intelligence (AI), a number of us have come to be frightened of large task variation, and for great factor. We understand that AI currently powers a lot of our favored applications and websites which, in the not so long run, AI will also be operating our cars, managing our work profiles, and also producing things we purchase.

About 50% of our work will, in truth, be taken over by AI and also automation within the following 10-15 years. As research suggests, the pace in which AI will replace jobs will only increase, affecting the highly educated and poorly enlightened alike.

While this is partly a warning of things to find, my genuine hope is to convey that there are still lots of crucial jobs that will be safe from AI infiltration. Bear in mind: AI is effective as well as versatile, but it can't do whatever that humans do. Below are a few of AI's weak points in work efficiency:

AI cannot create, conceive, or manage complex critical planning.
AI cannot achieve complicated work that requires specific hand-eye control.

AI cannot deal with unknown and unstructured spaces, specifically ones that it hasn't observed.

AI cannot, unlike human beings, communicate or feel with empathy and also compassion; therefore, it is not likely that people would go with connecting with a passive robot for typical interaction solutions. Given AI's limitations when it comes to carrying out humanistic tasks- jobs that are personal, innovative, and also compassionate-these are the tasks that will certainly be safe from variation. Most of these work will certainly call for a human-AI symbiosis, in which AI will certainly look after routine optimization tasks in tandem with humans, who will execute tasks that require warmth as well as empathy.

Right here is a list of occupations that will certainly be safe from AI in the next 5-10 years if you're worried concerning AI replacing your task.

Training/Tutoring
AI will be a great device for teachers and also educational organizations, as it will certainly help instructors figure out exactly how to customize educational program based on each student's competence, character, progression, as well as capacity. There will still be a wonderful need for human instructors in the future

Psychotherapy

Psychotherapy, community service, as well as marital relationship therapy are all professions that call for strong interaction abilities, compassion, as well as the capacity to win depend on from clients. These positions call for eager emotional intelligence, professionals who are qualified of communicating with people, gaming consoling clients in times of trauma, as well as offering long-term support. These are all bents machines.

Treatment

Dexterity is an obstacle for AI. These essential features of treatment make this career naturally humanistic, as well as not fit for AI.

Clinical treatment

The medical care sector is expected to grow considerably because of raised earnings, better health and wellness advantages, AI decreasing the price of treatment, and also a maturing populace who need more care. A lot of these variables will foster a symbiotic partnership in between humans and AI, which can assist with the analytical and also management aspects of medical care. Healthcare specialists like registered nurses and medical professionals will still be needed to carry out the attributes of care sustained by motivation, assistance, and also empathy.

AI-related research study and engineering

As AI innovation boosts, some entry-level AI positions will certainly also end up being automated. AI professionals will certainly require to maintain up with the changes caused by AI simply as, in recent years, software program designers have had to learn regarding setting up language, high-level language, object-oriented programming, mobile programs, as well as currently AI programming.

Fiction scripting

Narration needs one of the highest possible degrees of creativity, and one which AI will certainly have trouble to mimic. While AI will be able to compose social media messages, recommend book titles, as well as probably also copy writing designs, the ideal books, movies, and also plays will ultimately be written by humans, at the very least for the near future.

Protection law for Crimes

A lot of paralegal and primary job like record evaluation, evaluation, developing contracts, taking care of little situations, packaging instances, and coming up with suggestions can be done much better and also much more successfully with AI. The prices of legislation make it beneficial for AI companies to go after AI legal assistants and AI junior attorneys, but not leading legal representatives.

Engineering and Computer system/science

A big company report reveals that the variety of design experts like computer system researchers, engineers, IT admins, IT employees, and also technology consulters will increase by 20 million to 50 million worldwide by 2030. These work require remaining updated with technology as well as moving into areas that are not automated by modern technology.

Management Activities

Good managers have necessary human communication abilities including the capabilities to motivate, negotiate, and convince. They can effectively get in touch with staff members in behalf of firms. Much more importantly, the best managers are able to establish a strong office society as well as value system with their words and actions, which generates effort from their employees. While AI may be used to take care of efficiency, managerial job will remain to be accomplished by human beings. That stated, if a manager is just a bureaucrat resting behind a desk and giving workers orders, they will likely be changed by other people.

Science discipline

Science is the best career of human creative thinking. AI can just optimize based on goals set by human creative thinking. While AI is not likely to change researchers, AI would make wonderful devices for scientists. In drug exploration, AI can be made use of to hypothesize as well as test possible uses of recognized drugs for conditions, or filter feasible brand-new medicines for researchers to take into consideration. AI will certainly amplify human researchers.

There's no doubt that the AI transformation will require readjustments and an excellent offer of sacrifice, yet despairing as opposed to getting ready for what's to find is unproductive as well as, maybe, even reckless. We must keep in mind that our human propensity for empathy and also compassion is going to be a beneficial asset in the future workforce, and that work depended upon treatment, education and learning, as well as creative thinking, will certainly stay crucial to our culture.

Thus we have seen how AI will affect each and every aspect of our life especially jobs, driving/travelling. The initiative by OpenAI about practicing safe AI related activities should be followed by all organizations.

My friends working in top technology companies often described their AI experiences to me. One friend is working on Cortana in Microsoft U.S., another software engineer in Facebook U.S., and the other in Amazon Go and Google batchmates. They are very optimistic about the future of AI.

If you have any questions, suggestions, feedback, you can write to me at the contact details mentioned.

About me

The author is an IT Engineer from one of the topmost Engineering Institute (**VJTI**) where his final year project was based on IOT. He worked in Oracle, for clients like Sumitomo Bank and Silicon Valley Bank. He is a speaker on subjects like Chess and Mathematics. He would be coming up with a few books on AI based on his experience.

amazingpublishedbooks@gmail.com

Like Facebook page - "Artificial Intelligence Face Matching Page"

Linkedin - Akash

https://www.linkedin.com/in/akashitmanagerbusinessanalyst/

Bonus!

Wouldn't it be nice to know when my paperback books are launched at a discount? Well now is your chance!

Go to the below link For Instant Access!
http://

Simply as a 'Thank you for downloading this book, I would like to give you full access to an exclusive service that will email you notifications my paperback books are launched at a discount. If you are someone who is interested in saving money and getting technology books at a discount, then simple click the link for FREE access.

www.ingramcontent.com/pod-product-compliance
Lightning Source LLC
Chambersburg PA
CBHW071005050326
40689CB00014B/3500